KT-420-426

SLOT MACHINES

Dieter Ladwig

TIGER BOOKS INTERNATIONAL
LONDON

Translated by Phil Goddard
in association with First Edition Translations, Cambridge
Photography: Dieter Ladwig, Düsseldorf
Editor: Petra Raszkowski

CLB 3499
This edition published in 1994 by Tiger Books International PLC, London
by arrangement with CLB Publishing
© 1994 this English language edition CLB Publishing, Godalming, Surrey
Originally published in German by V.I.P.
© 1992 Paul Zsolnay Verlag Ges.m.b.H, Vienna
All rights reserved
Printed and bound in Italy
ISBN 1-85501-482-3

According to legend, the founding father of vending and slot machines was the Greek scientist, Hero, who invented a device selling "holy water" for five drachmas.

But the era of the slot machine began in the last quarter of the 19th century. We do not know where, when and by whom the first primitive slot machines, also known as nickel grinders or one-armed bandits, were produced. But we do know that the first counter-top models appeared around 1890. At the same time, floor machines were being designed: heavyweights which stood on the floor and were much more attractive than their table-top counterparts.

These primitive slot machines used three main systems of play. First there was the spinning wheel, a kind of vertical roulette. Then there were machines where the coins had to drop on a specific area to win, and thirdly there were machines which randomly paid out a specific percentage as soon as there were enough coins in the machine.

Even in these early days, frustrated gamblers unable to win the prizes they thought they deserved would sometimes cheat or even vent their rage on the machine. The counter-top machines still had to be monitored by staff, as they were only semi-automatic: only the floor machines were fully automatic and required no supervision.

The three great manufacturers of slot machines were the Mills Novelty Company, the Caille Brothers and the Watling Manufacturing Company. Between them, these companies dominated the market for 28 years. Others produced their own floor machines, but most were short-lived and were either taken over or forced out of business.

It was Mills that developed the extremely successful machine, "The Owl," but its biggest breakthrough came with the "Dewey." No other manufacturer sold as many machines as Mills.

The Caille brothers produced the "Puck," the "Eclipse," the "Centaur" and many other models, while Watling developed the "Big Six" and others. Later, a fourth manufacturer joined the Big Three: O.D. Jennings, who established his company as a major force in the market with its "Revamp" machines. He bought up slot machines which had either been pensioned off or banned by law, overhauled them and added his own cabinet and name.

Floor machines survived into the 1930s. Counter tops went out of fashion in the 1890s, but then enjoyed a revival in 1899, when Karl Fey, a German who had emigrated to the United States in 1882, produced the first "three-reel automatic payout machine" in San Francisco. This was the famous "Liberty Bell." Fey later changed his name to Charles after acquiring United States citizenship; the name "Liberty Bell" must have been in honor of his new homeland. These machines were set up in specially selected saloons in San Francisco, whose owners paid Fey a percentage of the takings. Mills made several attempts to buy out his rival, but Fey obstinately refused.

Although Fey made sure that his machines had a close eye kept on them, a "Liberty Bell" was stolen in 1905, probably by Mills. This marked the beginning of a run of ill-fortune for Charles Fey, who was really the inventor of the slot machine. First he lost his factory in the great San Francisco earthquake, and then he lost nearly all

his money when his bank went bankrupt.

In 1909, after four years of work, Mills brought out its own redesigned and technically improved "Liberty Bell." Inevitably, Thomas Watling and the Caille brothers then came out with their own "Liberty Bells," but Mills' model was by far the most successful. The "Operators Bell," developed in 1910, had a separate slot for ball gum, and the fruit symbols used today, such as lemons, oranges, cherries and plums, depicted the various flavors of gum.

The external design of Mills' "Bells" changed over the years. Initially the whole cabinet was made of metal, but later only the front was metal and the sides were made of oak. Later still, aluminum, the "magic metal," was used for the front. Each time such an innovation was introduced it was immediately copied by all its competitors, with scant disregard for the law on such matters. Inevitably, there were several legal cases.

In 1926 Jennings, the country's biggest second-hand dealer in used slot machines, began designing and manufacturing its own machines. The first of these was the "Bantam," so called because of its relatively small size.

In 1929 the Big Four became the Big Five as a new manufacturer, Ed Pace, entered the market in a big way. Pace and the juke box company Rock-Ola scored a huge success with the production of "conversion fronts." These new fronts, with a jackpot and vending facility, led to a new boom in the industry. Selling chewing gum was a subtle way of getting round gambling laws, as technically they were vending rather than gambling machines. These combination fronts, and the fact that patents to the individual machines were not very clear, meant that there was soon a huge variety of machines on the market. This sometimes makes it difficult today to establish which companies made which machines.

The slot machine manufacturers were hit by the depression of the 1930s, but most managed to keep their heads above water by producing cheaper machines and getting round the gambling laws. This book shows some of the many models and variations produced during this time. Manufacturers had many ups and downs, especially with the arrival of war, which forced many of them to stop or cut back production of gaming machines. But some of the leading names managed to come bouncing back.

The next setback they faced were new gambling laws, including the Johnson Act of 1951. This law meant that the only remaining markets were Nevada and the export market, both of which became extremely competitive as a result. The Caille brothers ceased production, and the Big Five became the Big Four again. Jennings was still thriving with its "Chief" range, and Mills was the market leader with its successful "Hi-Top Line." Watling sold all its rights to European companies; shortly afterwards Pace shut down production, and finally Mills went into liquidation. It was the end of an era.

Last time I went to Las Vegas I found that the Antique Slot-Machine Museum no longer existed. So this book is intended as a homage to these old slot machines, a Hall of Fame for all the classic and beautifully designed machines of yesteryear.

Jennings **Chiefs** approx. 1955

Jennings "Chiefs" were used in casinos and clubs, with the name of the club appearing on the machine. This machine, for example, was operated by the Nevada Club.

This machine may not have scored very highly in the style stakes, but is still fondly remembered by Americans who were around in the immediate post-war period. The machine required very little maintenance, and was sold in many other countries from 1946 onwards as the "Export Chief," converted for a variety of currencies. The "Export Chief" is not hugely popular among collectors, though connoisseurs say it has an unusual payout mechanism. The machine is almost identical to the 1945 "Lucky Chief."

Jennings
Buckaroo
Four Reels
1955

This new member of the "Sun Chief" family was launched as the first post-war, four-reel machine in 1955. When four "Buckaroo" symbols were lined up this machine paid out $250, and the jackpot was up to $5,000. The Nevada Club in Reno, North Virginia, featured this Jennings as its star attraction on New Year's Eve, 1955, and of course made a great deal of money from it.

Jennings
Golden
Nugget
1950

This machine was modified for the Golden Nugget Casino in Las Vegas. The two golden female figures also feature on the Mills "Golden Nugget."

Jennings
Sweepstake Chief
1950

Between 1945 and 1950, Jennings brought out around ten basic models with a number of variations. Money flowed freely in the United States after the years of wartime privation.

Buckley
Bones
1935-1939

The "Bones Counter Dice" is much coveted by collectors and fetches high prices. It is an automatic dice game that pays out money. Forgotten until recently, it is very unusual both for the dice aspect and for its sophisticated mechanism. The Bally "Reliance" machine is almost identical and was built by the same manufacturer, but does not fetch the same high prices among collectors.

Jennings **Super De Luxe Club Chief** 1946

This was the first illuminated slot machine, and was a companion model to the "Standard Chief." The symbols in the top right and top left are highly distinctive. The names of the many Jennings "Chiefs" are often somewhat confusing. The first real post-war machine was the "Club Chief," of which more than 200,000 were sold; there was also a "De Luxe Club Chief" with a number of different coin slots. These mechanisms were still being used almost unchanged in the 1960s.

Improved Century Vendor Bell Machine

1933-1935

To paraphrase Shakespeare, the names of Jennings machines were full of sound and fury, signifying nothing. The "Improved Century" appeared in the same year as the ordinary "Century," the only difference being its more elaborate art deco design. The old-fashioned design of the ordinary "Century" hardly reflected the motto of the Chicago World's Fair in 1933: "The Century of Progress." There were 28 variations of the machine illustrated here, including mint vendors with twin, triple or reserve jackpots.

Mills **Heros** approx. 1930

The "Heros" was produced by Mills in the US for the German market, and distributed by Rhein-Ruhr-Automaten in Düsseldorf. The machines were rebuilt and redesigned to suit European tastes; the reels bore numbers rather than fruit symbols, and there was a different reward system with no jackpot. The reels took around 15 seconds to come to a stop, unlike the machine's American counterpart which took only 3-5 seconds. The machine also included mint vendors, but these were not used in Germany. In 1935, the machines were banned by the Hitler regime.

Watling
1924 O.K.
Operator Bell Eagle
1923-1926

Watling was well known as a copycat, and here again it shamelessly imitated one of its competitors. Even collectors sometimes confuse it with the Mills "Operators Bell" of 1915-1922: the only difference between the two is that the Watling has an eagle at the top and the Mills has an owl.

Although Watling tried to establish the machine under the name of "Twentieth Century," it was better known under its nickname of "Eagle." A number of minor cosmetic changes were made to the front in 1926, and the Watling "Eagle" became the Watling "Lincoln De Luxe."

Mills
Commercial
1905

Card machines were particularly popular with operators and players alike at this time. Each machine cost just over $40, and around 10,000 are believed to have been sold in California alone in the space of five years. The prize for a royal flush was a hundred cigars.

Mills
Tura
1930

This machine was built in the United States, probably by Mills, for a company called Schwarz in Leipzig, Germany. The chewing gum and peppermint vendors were not used and therefore covered over with mirrors. The machines were banned by the Nazis in 1935. Schwarz also built its own machines under license.

Jennings
Automatic Counter Vendor Display Front
1925

The predecessor of this machine was the Jennings "Automatic Mint Vendor" of 1923. The only visual difference was the bottom front section, which was made of wood rather than the metal used in the Mint Vendor. Jennings was the first manufacturer to replace ball gum with peppermints, and also removed all references to rewards from the machine to give it the appearance of a pure vending machine. The large vendor display front complete with candies and the "future pay" system all gave this machine an air of absolute legality.

Jennings
Today Vendor
with jackpot, 1929

The Jennings "Today Vendor" of 1926, which used the "future pay" system as an ostensibly legal form of gambling, was the predecessor of this machine. It paid out "amusement tokens" together with packs of peppermints. Here again, Jennings used Dutch figures and carnations in its front design.

Penny Ball Gum Vendor

1926

This machine was built as an amusement vendor, gambling slot and fortune-teller, and was described in its advertising as "three machines in one." Slot machine manufacturers also sold their own gum, for example 16 1/2 cents for a packet of 100 balls. If you bought 2,500 boxes of 100, the price was reduced to 13 1/2 cents, but that meant you had 250,000 gum balls in stock. Which was a lot of chewing!

Mills Pace **Conversion Front** 1930 onwards

A fine 1930s machine with mint vendors on either side and the jackpot in the center.

Known by collectors as the "Cherry Front," this machine from the "Rol-A-Top" family was mouth-wateringly decorated with gleaming red cherries: a veritable feast for the eyes. The triple jackpot combination was conspicuously visible almost at eye height. Here again, the "Fabulous Original Rol-A-Top Escalator" was placed immediately under the coin slot. Not surprisingly, there were a number of different versions of the Two Column Front Vendor.

Watling
Rol-A-Top
1935

Watling was constantly creating new variations in the "Rol-A-Top" series. This one had a coin front at the top, a double jackpot and two mint vendors. Watling was based at 4640-4660 West Fulton Street in Chicago.

Watling
Rol-A-Top Checkerboard
1947

This was Watling's last slot machine, which borrowed the distinctive design of the 1933 Mills "Mystery Castle Front." Watling sold its stock of machines to England after new anti-gambling laws were passed in the US. Pace ceased production at the same time, and Mills went into liquidation in 1953: two more slot machine giants had quit the battlefield.

Watling
Rol-A-Top
1935

Watling
Rol-A-Top
Bird of Paradise
1936

The hearts of slot machine collectors miss a beat when they see this machine. All the machines in the "Rol-A-Top" range are unusually attractive, but this must be the most eye-catching of them all. The front has the same eagle below a colorful array of fruit; originally known as the "Rol-A-Tor," this machine's name had to be changed because it had already been trademarked by another company.

The "Rol-A-Top" is a highly unusual design, with the pile of imitation gold coins providing the player with a hint of vast riches to come. I believe it is by far one of the most original machines made by this manufacturer. The eagle keeps a beady eye on twin jackpots nos. 1 and 2, with the coins designed to encourage players to put another nickel in the slot. This model is very much in demand by collectors, mainly because of the relatively rare "Circular Coin Escalator."

Jennings Silver Moon Chief 1938

The "Chief" series went into production in 1938 and sold particularly well, so over the years, as with Watling's "Rol-A-Top" range, the manufacturer simply placed different cabinets on identical machines. Later models using the same mechanism included the "Sportsman," "Sky Chief" and "Bronze Chief." During the war, Jennings also produced a version of the "Victory Chief" with a wooden cabinet, known as the "Wooden Indian." This machine has never become really popular with collectors.

Jennings **Victory Chief** 1942

Although Jennings made widespread use of Indian imagery in their "Chief" range, the "Victory Chief" was an exception. As this model was produced during the war, it includes a soldier blowing the trumpet to herald victory, patriotically accompanied by the American Eagle. The "Victory Chief" was a derivative of the "Bronze Chief" of the previous year, but instead of the Indian's head it bore an eagle, and the two stars were replaced by two trumpets. Like fast food, fast design was very much an American invention.

Jennings **Sportsman** 1938

Golf, tennis, archery, ten-pin bowling, swimming and shooting all featured on this machine. The designers were clearly thinking of the Olympic adage that it is better to play than to win – it doesn't matter how good a sportsman or woman you are; you can't beat the machine!

Mills Golden Nugget approx. 1947-1955

This machine is one of the many conversions of the Mills "Jewel Bell," and was also known as "Golden Doll." The Golden Nugget casino in Los Angeles wanted its own distinctively designed slot machines, and a number of versions of this model were built as a result. Reproduction "Golden Nuggets" are a common sight on the collectors" market.

Mills/Sheffler **Star** 1939

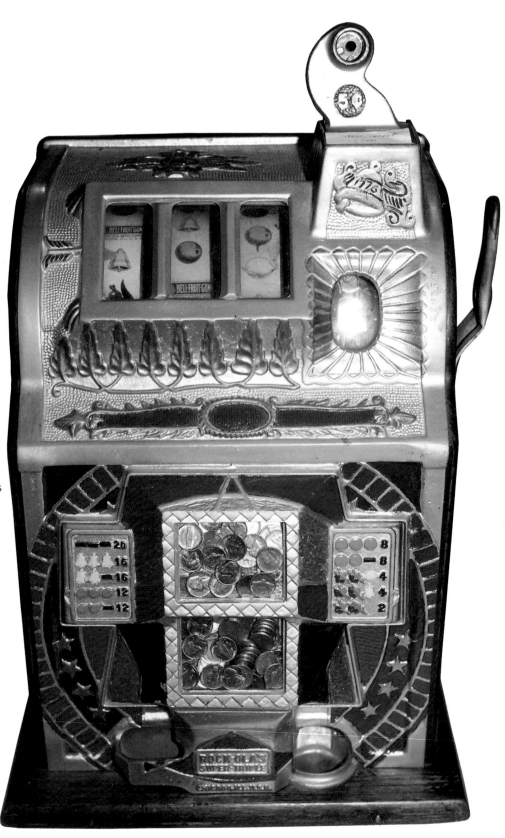

Rock-Ola, better known as a
music box manufacturer, also
produced jackpot fronts for
existing machines; hence the
name Rock-Ola on the front.
This model was also available as
a vendor.

Jennings **Four Star Chief** 1936

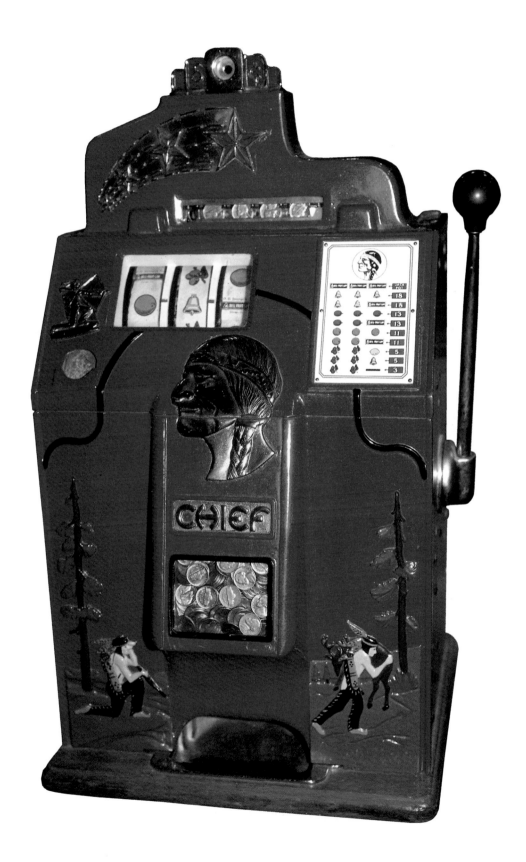

The "Four Star Chief" was a beautifully designed machine with Indian hunting scenes and a background of pines. The name of the machine is also embodied in the four stars underneath the coin slot. The "Four Star Chief" was also available as a vendor.

Mills **Bonus Bell** 1937

This machine was also known as "Horse Head," for obvious reasons. If the word "Bonus" appeared in the window, the machine paid an additional 18 coins. The bonus was designed to generate repeat business and customer loyalty, but its one drawback was a very complicated mechanism which often led to incorrect payouts. The "Horse Head" is one of the "Silent Bells" series developed in 1931 by the four sons of Herbert S. Mills. The series was a major advance both in terms of its mechanism and its appearance.

Mills Silent Golden Bell 1932

This one-armed bandit is better known as the "Roman Head." The "Silent Golden" came from the quiet mechanism and the golden features of the Roman youth on the front. The design also includes two Roman Graces pouring liberal amounts

of wine and coins onto the ground. If three "Gold Award" symbols appeared together, the machine would pay out the jackpot. The beautifully designed front, with its symbolic representation of the nature of money, has made this machine a coveted collector's piece.

Jennings **One Star Chief** 1935

This machine was the forerunner of the "Four Star Chief" of 1936. The Indian's successful hunt for wild animals is presumably intended to symbolize the gambler's quest for riches. This one-armed bandit was also available as a vendor; the only difference was the addition of three stars and two pines, and a new model was born.

Mills/Pace **Jackpot** 1932

The lower front of this slot machine is very similar to that of the "Twin Jackpot Conversion" produced by Fey in 1932. The owner of this machine clearly did not make a very good job of removing the copper deposits created by the coins.

The slot machine market was highly competitive in the early '30s, and there were many technical innovations during this period, including the "Electrovendor," "Twin Play" and "Baby Grand." But the invention of the Jackpot in 1927 was the most important of these innovations, and Mills and Jennings began making jackpot machines in 1928. However, Rock-Ola was still the market leader in jackpot fronts.

Mills **Extrabell Aitkens Front** 1946

Slot machine manufacturers were affected by shortages of materials in the immediate post-war period, and so they overhauled old, pre-war machines and fitted them with new cabinets. One of the results was this beautiful "Extrabell Aitkens Front," which cost $77.50.

Jennings The Joker 1953-1958

In 1951, Congress passed the Johnson Act banning all one-armed bandits. The Act proved a disaster for the slot machine industry: in California, for example, there was a $500 fine per machine. In 1953 Taylor & Co. of Chicago circumvented the Act by producing a machine with no coin slot and marked "For Amusement Only." No money went into or out of the machine: instead customers paid the attendant or bartender first, and he or she switched the machine on from behind the counter and paid out any winnings. Jennings was one of Taylor's major customers, and used the system in their "Chief" series. The new machine was appropriately called "The Joker:" it had outwitted the long arm of the law.

Pace **All Star Comet Bell Machine** 1936-1939

„The Heart Of The Slot"

This machine was a departure from Pace's previously very conservative designs. Operators called it simply the "1936 Comet," but it later became known by slot machine historians as the "Blue Front." There were a number of versions of this model: it was available as a vendor, in variations accepting coins from 1 to 50 cents, and also in a different color as the "Orange Front."

Mills **Liberty Bell** 1909

The first "Liberty Bell" was introduced by Charles Fey in 1899, and was followed by Mills' version in 1909. The mechanism was almost identical: only the external appearance of the machine had significantly changed. During the next fifty years, a total of around a million "Bell Machines" were sold.

Mills Jackpot Bell Machine Poinsettia 1928-1931

This machine was used in many Las Vegas clubs in the 1930s. It was the most successful of the Mills "Jackpot" series, and was available in a number of versions. One was decorated with two torches and was known as the "Torch," or "Torch Bullseye"; another had two coin dispensers.

Jennings
Little Duke
1932

The "Little Duke" from Jennings' "Royal Family" is a very interesting machine. It was very popular among players in the 1930s, and has since become much in demand by collectors. More conservative gamblers liked the fact that it took pennies, nickels or dimes, and operators liked it because it was cheaper and smaller than other machines. The machine had three spinning wheels and an art deco design, and was also available as a gum vendor.

Jennings Pace
Star Revamp Bell Machine
1933-1937

Pace was second only to Rock-Ola as the biggest manufacturer of jackpot fronts. Pace also made fronts in Mills, Jennings and Watling versions and sold them to operators of older machines to update them; hence the name "Revamp." Although the machine illustrated here looks like a Pace "Comet" at first sight and was known as a Pace "Star Revamp Bell," it is actually a Jennings "Operators Bell" from the 1920s. The front was originally designed by Charles Fey, who used it in the Fey "Twin Jackpot Conversion" machine of 1932. It was also produced and sold by companies in Wisconsin and elsewhere, and was available in many different versions.

Mills
Jackpot Front Vendor Bell Machine
1930-1933

This machine was derived from the two top sellers of the late 1920s: the "Jackpot" and the "Front O.K. Vendor." It had vendors on either side for rolls of mints, and the relatively small jackpot was decorated with symbolic flashes of lightning. The curved gooseneck coin slot and bullseye coin detector are typical of slot machines from this period. In its brochure, Mills said: "The Vendor is a noteworthy example of harmony in design and balance. It is compact and solid in appearance ...." The company had scored another success with this machine, and this was reflected in the sales figures.

Mills
Cherry Bell
Bursting Cherry
1937

The "Cherry" derived its name mainly from the fact that it paid out double (ten coins instead of five) when two cherries and a bell or lemon were visible in the window. This machine had an additional jackpot, and was nicknamed the "Exploding Cherry." The Mills "Brown Front Bell" of 1938 was very similar to the "Cherry Bell," with the only difference being the brown background and orange center. These machines were also made with a sword on the mint vendor on the right-hand side. All these models are highly popular with collectors.

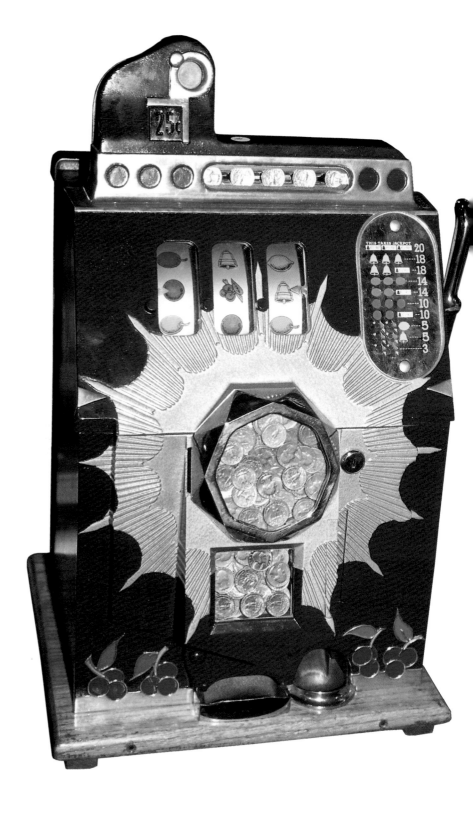

Mills
Brown
Front Bell
1938

Buckley Criss Cross Bell 1948-1955

This machine was patented after Mills' "Black Cherry" and "Golden Falls" series appeared, and bore some similarities to them. It was very popular with gamblers, as its "Tic-Tac-Toe" system gave a good chance of winning.

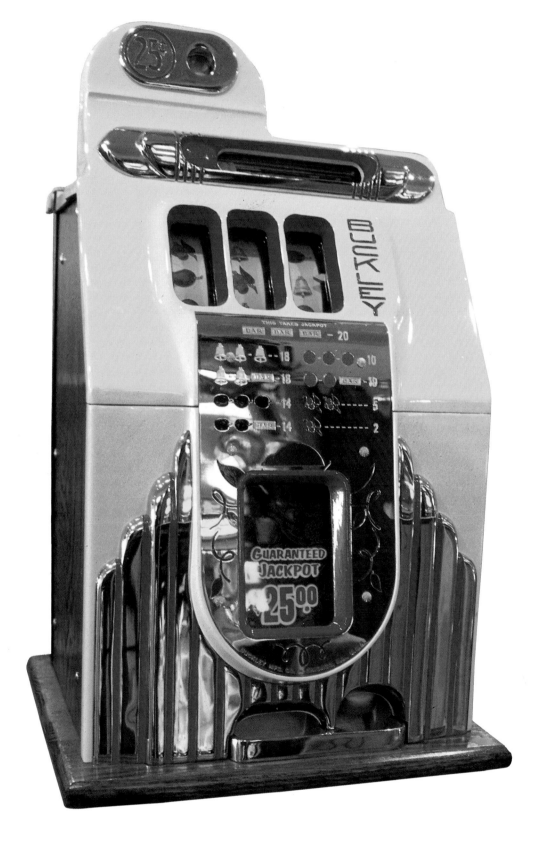

Caille
New Century Puck Floor Machine
1901-1917

The Caille brothers of Detroit produced the "Puck" line very successfully for many years. These Caille floor machines are now coveted by collectors and fetch high prices. The name "New Century" was used not only for slot machines, but for almost anything new produced around the turn of the century. The Puck's metal decoration was available in either nickel plate or antique copper. The machine shown here dates from 1901 and is based on the 1898 "Puck," but with an improved mechanism and styling. The machine made inroads into the market share achieved by the more successful Mills "Dewey."

Caille **Mixed Triplet** approx. 1903-1916

This imposing Caille floor machine was a classic of its kind. The idea of combining two, or in this case, three machines into one was a way of getting round taxes and license fees charged on slot machines. The Caille brothers were the most successful manufacturers of these triplets, which were also sold in much smaller numbers by Watling, Mills and Victor. The machine here weighs around 600 pounds and is 5 feet 6 inches long: it consists of a Caille "Eclipse" and "Centaur," and a Watling "Big Six." The Mills "Dewey" triplets were even bigger: they were 8 inches taller, 7 feet 6 inches long and weighed in at 900 pounds. This was obviously a

drawback, as they were difficult to move and could not be quickly turned to face the wall in the event of a police raid. This Caille "Mixed Triplet" is the essence of pure nostalgia.

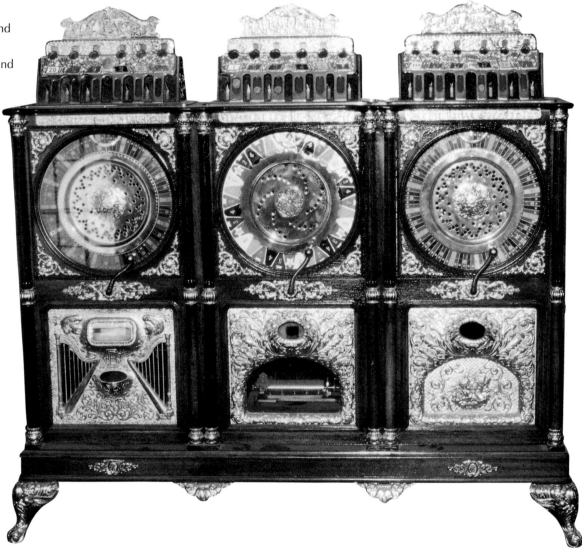

The name "Judge" was
purloined from Caille-Schiemer:
Mills was not averse to a bit of
copying. The mechanism of this
machine came from the
successful "Owl." There was
also a "Twin-Line," which was a
combination of two machines,
the "Owl" and the "Judge."

Mills **Dewey** 1899-1929

The "Dewey" was named after Admiral George E. Dewey, who inflicted a devastating defeat on the Spanish fleet in the Battle of Manila Bay, in the Spanish-American War of 1898. On his return he was feted as a hero, and H.S. Mills jumped on the bandwagon by naming his machine after the admiral. Various changes were made to the cabinet, the spinning wheel and the metal ornaments over the years, and there are believed to have been twelve versions in all, one of them with music. This was a common method of evading the law in "Closed Towns" where gambling was forbidden. A music box was installed, the machine bore a plaque saying "Musical Cabinet," and the lawmakers at least temporarily turned a blind eye. Of course the sound reproduction left a great deal to be desired, but nobody cared: this was a gambling machine pure and simple.

Mills **Owl Floor Machine** 1897-1918

This machine was designed by Herbert S. Mills' father, and sold by his son's company; the owl was the company's trademark. Ten thousand of these machines are believed to have been sold at $150 each. When excellent copies of the machine began appearing on the market, Mills cut the price to less than $100. Around 15 to 20 other manufacturers made their own versions of "The Owl." The one pictured here is definitely a Mills – or so I have been reliably informed.

This machine was named after Detroit, the city where Caille-Schiemer had its factory before its name was changed to Caille. This 1899 model is simply designed, without the elaborate, somewhat tacky metal trimmings and ornate legs of later models. The lyres depicted on either side emphasize the ostensibly musical nature of this machine.

Further proof of Watling's ability to produce flawless copies of other people's machines is evident in this version of a Mills "Chicago." Watling made no bones about the fact that this was a copy, especially as his company had never produced a

machine called the "Chicago," which he now claimed to have improved. Watling's version cost between $75 and $100, depending on the coins it took: the higher value the stake, the more the machine cost. If you wanted a machine with music, it would cost you another $20. There were also twin and triplet versions of the "Improved Chicago."

This Chicago company, founded by John Gabel, used a slightly similar design to the highly successful Mills "Owl" series, and also produced its own machine under the name of "The Owl." However the "Star" shown here had a different mechanism to Mills' machines. John Gabel also made the "Fox" and the "Musical Fox" before later moving out of the slot machine business; he was also responsible for the first "music box" on the market. The wheel was an integral part of the cabinet.

Mills **Silent War Eagle** 1931-1944

Mills originally began selling this machine under the name of "Bell Machine," but it very soon became known as the "War Eagle." Mills' four sons developed the "Silent Bell" range after his death and began a trend which lasted many years: the "Silent Bell" machines combined a quiet and very reliable mechanism with beauty and elegance. The "War Eagle" is therefore very much a collector's piece, worth very much more than its original price of $76.50. Its technology was used successfully, and with only minor changes, for 35 years. The first version of the "War Eagle" had two jackpots: later there was only one larger jackpot. Between 1942 and 1945 the "War Eagle" was available in chrome, gold chrome and copper chrome versions.

Groetchen
Columbia
1939-1950

Jennings
Challenger Console Bell
1947-1955

This popular and enjoyable machine had two coin slots and two jackpots. One added attraction that made it stand out from the crowd was its electric lighting.

This machine was very much smaller and more compact than traditional slot machines, and incorporated a number of technical innovations, including the coin storage mechanism. It was also harder to cheat the machine with its last in, first out coin system. The "Columbia" could also be very quickly converted by the operator. Once again, there were many different versions, including the "Gold Award Columbia," the "Columbia Standard," "Columbia Separator" and "Twin Jackpot Columbia." Another factor in the machine's favor was that it was 50 to 70 percent cheaper than the standard prices of other slot machines.

Hi Top Line
1947-1962

Counter O.K. Bell Machine
1929-1932

The "O.K." was invented by Watling. It was a versatile machine which could also be used as a vendor, and gained its name from the manufacturer's claim that it was legally OK. This was an extremely successful model, though it is very rare nowadays because so many were destroyed by the authorities. The side vendor machine shown below remains just a dream for most collectors.

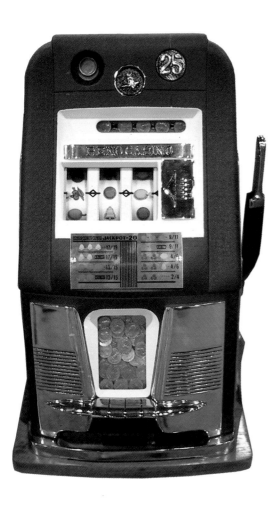

This model, built for the Reno Casino, was part of a series of different Mills machines from the "Criss Cross" and "777" series of "Hi-Tops," which lasted for fifteen years. These machines are still used in casinos around the world, very often with their original cabinet.

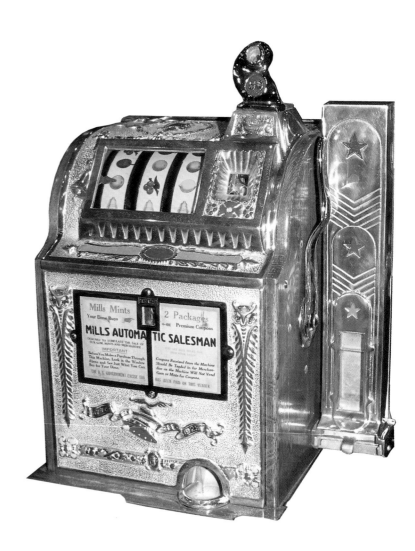

Bally Reliance Dice Machine 1935-1937

This unusual slot machine was made both for Bally and Buckley by a subcontractor. The first time the handle was pulled, the first drum began rotating and threw two dice in the upper window. If they totalled a certain score, such as 7 or 11, the machine paid two coins. If the score was 2, 3 or 12, the game ended; if the score was anything else, the player was given another pull of the handle. The dice were thrown again, and again either the game ended or the player was given more throws of the dice. An added incentive to play was the $5 bonus in tokens in the left-hand box. These machines were almost unknown in the 1970s, but then a number were mysteriously offered to collectors in their original packing, with no-one quite certain where they came from. Nowadays, both the Bally "Reliance" and Buckley "Bones" fetch a king's ransom.

Groetchen **Ball Gum** or **Tavern** 1935

After the ending of Prohibition, this machine provided a small and not entirely legal boost to bar takings, with a penny stake and rewards of ball gum and free drinks. This machine cost only $15, and paid out a miserly 45 percent.

Mills
Black Cherry
1945

The "Black Cherry," named after its five cherry symbols, is a good machine to start a collection with. This was Mills' first post-war gaming machine, built on the simple principle of taking a 1939 "Chrome Bell" and replacing the diamonds with cherries to create a new machine. Simple!

Mills
Futurity with Side Vendor
1936

The "Futurity" had a number of unusual features which proved popular with gamblers. There's nothing worse than playing for ages and not winning a cent, but this was not a problem with this machine. Every tenth time the handle was pulled there was a guaranteed win or your money was paid back. There were also a number of ways of winning a few nickels, and so this machine was very customer-friendly. This may have been the reason why electric versions of the machine were still popular in the 1960s.

Mills
Screen Stars
approx. 1940

This unusual machine paid out
on the names of film stars
instead of lemons, plums and
cherries. The figure at the
bottom is an Oscar.

There were a number of
different models in the Mills "Hi-
Top" series, and in all around
120,000 were sold during their
20-year history.

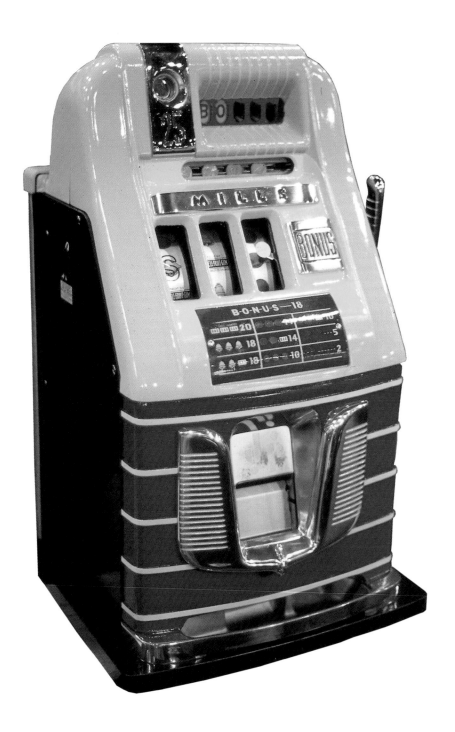

Watling
Rol-A-Top
Bird of Paradise
1936

This beautiful Watling from the "Rol-A-Top" series is one of the most expensive of all slot machines, and is rarely seen on the market today.

Pace
De Luxe Chrome Bell
1945

There were only two differences between this and the pre-war, 1939 model: the later machine had chrome side panels, and the win symbols included "buy," "keep" and "bond." This is an example of the trend in the late 1930s towards much more streamlined designs.

Crown
1940

I found this Australian slot machine in the United States: it probably dates from the 1940s. Despite its very attractive design and use of playing cards as win symbols, it does not seem to have found favor with American collectors. The first "poker machines" appeared on the Australian market as early as 1898. In 1953, after slot machines were legalized, Ainsworth Aristocrat began producing them.

Fancy Front Comet

1935

The name "Fancy Front" was well deserved by this colorful and elaborately designed machine. Its double jackpot and circular coin escalator are a feast for the eyes, whether you're a collector or not. Pace introduced the "Comet" in 1932 as its answer to the Mills "Silent Bells" series.

Pace

Bantam Gum Vendor

1932

Ed Pace was a former Mills employee who was a dealer in used one-armed bandits for many years. He brought out his first "Bell Machine" in 1927, a small, lightweight machine ideally suited to the Depression years as it was very inexpensive and paid out up to 70 percent. Ed Pace had correctly judged the mood of the times, and his company rapidly became one of the slot machine giants.

Watling
Treasury
1936

This was a companion model to the "Rol-A-Top." With its distinctive gooseneck and front richly decorated with gold coins, it was based on the "Blue Seal" range. The sign stating "No Gambling Allowed On This Machine" was yet another charade designed to get round the gaming laws. But diehard gamblers went on pouring their coins into the slot, oblivious to such legal niceties.

Pace
Comet Bell
1932-1935

The machine shown here is a typical example of the many different designs and widespread copying of the time. The owner thought it was a Pace "Fancy Front," but I discovered that the lower front comes from the 1932 Mills Pace "Jackpot;" the Jennings Pace "Jackpot" from the same year has a similar design. The top comes from the 1935 Pace "Fancy Front," which is very similar to the 1933-1937 Pace "Star Revamp Bell." Put these facts together, and the solution is that this machine is a Pace "Comet Bell" dating from 1932-1935, with a rotary coin escalator and double jackpot, not to mention a highly attractive color scheme. Even US experts sometimes find it difficult to identify machines from this era: even during this short four-year period many changes, often very minor, were made to this machine.

Mills created a classic with this machine from the "Hi Top" series, and it is still very popular among collectors. The "Hi Tops" are probably the most confusingly varied of any range of machines, partly because Mills produced huge numbers of variations and partly because it was so widely copied by Buckley and other lesser manufacturers. The slot machine industry was gripped by copying fever until the 1950s.

Pace
Bantam Jackpot Bell
1931-1935

In 1928, Pace began its first large-scale production with the "Bantam" series, which sold very well for eight years. This particular "Bantam" is undoubtedly one of the most attractive in the series, with its rising sun symbol marking Pace's fortunes – or was it a setting sun reflecting the player's declining bank balance?

Burtmier
Pony Bell Machine
1934-1935

Burtmier produced two versions of this "Pony:" a "Bell Machine" and a side vendor. The twin jackpot was nothing unusual, what is different is that the machine had two reels of fruit symbols instead of three. It was called the "Pony" because of its relatively compact size and its weight of only about 33 lb. The doyen of slot machine collectors, Roy Arrington of Las Vegas, tells me that the name Burtmier comes from that of its president – Burt Chochran – and one of the company's secretaries, whose name was Meyer.

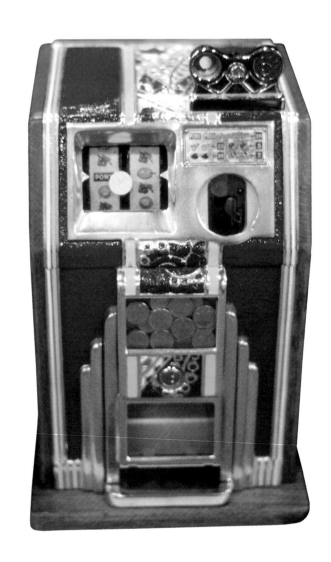

The machine pictured here was specially designed for nightclubs but was not particularly successful, perhaps because it was so expensive. This high price was because mint vendors often had to be removed from drugstores, bars and other public places on legal grounds. There were nickel, quarter and half-dollar versions of the "Console Chief," and it used the mechanism of the "Four Star Chief."

This "bandit" was developed for the Chicago World's Fair in 1933. The motto of the fair was "The Century of Progress," and this machine had an unusually advanced design for its time. It was available in 5, 10 and 25-cent versions, and as a side and front vendor.

Mystery Blue Front
Bell Castle Front

1933-1943

More than 50,000 of these machines are believed to have been built, which would make it the biggest-selling slot machine of all time. As usual, there were many different versions: the one here is a side vendor, with the sword above the side vendor matching the heraldic motif on the front. The name "Mystery" derives from the fact that the machine occasionally dispensed random amounts of money that were not shown on the reward card.

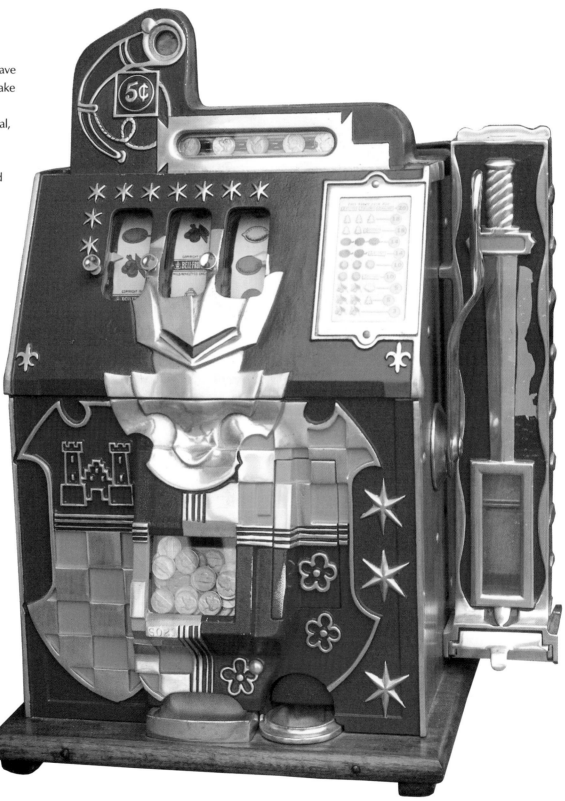

A.C. Novelty
Multi Bell Seven Way
1937

Adolph Caille, the last of the Caille brothers, sold the company to Fuller Johnson in 1932. Later, however, he went back into the slot machine business and set up a new company, A.C. Novelty, with his son Arthur. He decided to design a revolutionary new seven-coin slot machine, and the result was the "Multi Bell." Shortly afterwards Adolph Caille died, and Arthur sold out to Buckley. With the "Multi Seven" the player could put coins in any combination of the seven slots. The stop position of the first reel showed the win symbol, and the third reel the number of coins inserted. If three win symbols appeared, the gambler won one of the seven jackpots; hence the second part of the machine's name.

Watling
Blue Seal
1929-1935

This may not be the most visually striking of machines, but collectors say it is a particularly reliable one. The "Blue Seal" series appeared on the market in 1927; if you tell a collector you've got a "Blue Seal" they'll automatically ask you which one: there were countless different versions on the market.

Mills
Operators Bell
1916-1923

The "Operators Bell" was similar to the 1915 model, and went on being built until late 1922. People in the Roaring Twenties were in constant quest of new forms of entertainment and, as the market leader in slot machines, Mills was well equipped to meet this need. The machines were also installed in drugstores and soft drink parlors, mostly with the obligatory mint vendors. Mills began making machines from the magic metal, aluminum, in the early 1920s. The famous Mills owl appears in slightly changed form on either side of the machine.

Jennings
Jackpot
Bell Dutch Boy
1929-1931

The Caille brothers were highly successful with their "Jackpot Bell" machines: Mills followed suit, and Jennings produced their own versions shortly afterwards. The Dutch boys are shown wearing yellow clogs and distinctive caps. There were a number of versions of this machine, also known by its nickname of "Blue Boy."

Caille
Silent Sphinx Bell
1932

Worried by the success of Mills' "Silent Bell Machines" with their quiet mechanism, Caille also tried to reduce the noise level of their machines, but were never wholly successful in doing so. The "Silent Sphinx" was intended to compete with Mills visually, if not aurally, and was available in three- and four-reel versions, and as a ball gum vendor. In the same year, 1932, Adolph Caille finally closed down the company, so the "Sphinx" was Caille Brothers' last machine, a highly elegant piece of slot machine history.

Caille
Superior Jackpot Bell Machine
1928-1932

Caille identified a market trend and modified the "Superior Naked Lady" to make the "Superior Jackpot." In terms of design and attractiveness, this machine undoubtedly features very high on the list of the Top 100 Most Popular Machines, and many US collectors regard it as an absolute must. Although many other slot machines featured jackpots, the Caille "Superior" was probably the most popular machine of its time.

Caille
Superior Naked Lady
1926-1931

The name of this model was something of a change of direction for Caille. "Operator" and "Bell" were too obviously references to gaming machines, and so the new name of "Superior" was chosen. Adolph Caille had invented his new "slug-proof coin detector" in 1925, and this was built into the "Naked Lady." This machine gave a much-needed boost to the company's fortunes in a market which was extremely competitive. Today, it is every collector's dream to own one.

Mills
Baseball Vendor
1929

Slot machine manufacturers were constantly looking for new ways of getting round anti-gambling laws. At first sight, the "Baseball Vendor" was purely designed for amusement: the reels bore pictures of balls, players, gloves and flags, and the machine paid out tokens and the obligatory mints. The Mills Owl kept a beady eye on events and kept its thoughts about the true nature of the machine to itself. This popular game was inevitably copied by Jennings and Watling. The "Baseball Vendor" was a very attractive and unusual slot machine, and still exists in many collections.

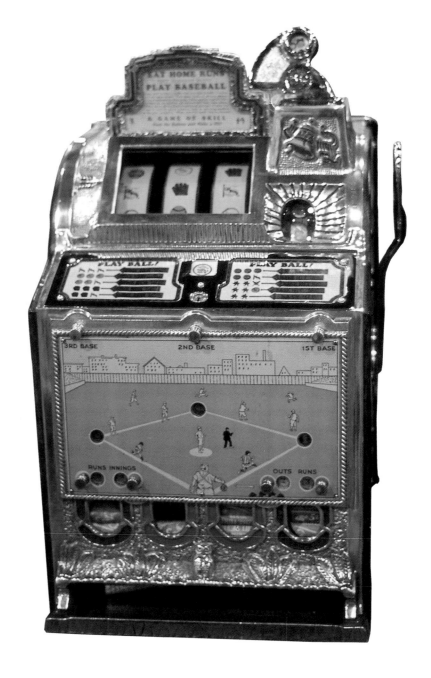

Mills **Chrome Bell Diamond Front** 1933-1944

The name "Chrome Bell" comes from the fact that this machine originally came with a chrome front. It acquired the nickname "Diamond Front" from the ten gold diamonds which promised untold wealth. The machine had a very reliable mechanism and sold very well. This was the first time that Mills had used chrome in its designs and, probably as a result, it was regarded as the most attractive machine on the market in 1939. The series also included slightly altered models such as the "Gold Chrome," "Emerald Chrome" and "Copper Chrome."

Pace **Comet** approx. 1939

This model was made of wood, but had the same design as the Pace "De Luxe Chrome Bell." This machine shows what a good combination wood and chrome can make.

Jennings **Operators Bell** approx. 1920

O.D. Jennings, born in Kentucky in 1874, very soon became one of the big names in the slot machine business. He began work as a salesman with Mills, but soon realized the potential of the market and set up his own company, Industrial Novelty Works, in 1906. He bought machines at rock bottom prices in states where they had been banned, overhauled them and made various technical changes, and then added new fronts with his name on them. This turned into a big business, and before very long Jennings was making high-quality products which proved very popular with players and operators alike until well into the 1960s.

Jennings
Prospector
1946

This machine's Wild West name was meant to evoke the possibility of vast wealth and the excitement of prospecting for gold.

Jennings **Duchess** 1933

The 1932 "Little Duke" inevitably spawned a "Duchess," which came out in 1933. Many collectors regard the "Duchess" as an essential part of the Royal Family. Like the "Little Duke," the "Duchess" was a compact machine, its price highly competitive by 1933 standards.

Caille
Ben Hur Counter Machine
1908-1932

When Caille introduced the first machines of this type in 1908, they were advertised as "the smallest slot machines with automatic payout." They cost between $50 and $60 and are coveted collectors' pieces today.

Jennings Rock-Ola **Reserve** 1930

David C. Rock-Ola, who also made music boxes, weighing scales and pinball machines, was one of the leading manufacturers of the new and extremely popular jackpot fronts. Here, one of his creations appears on a Jennings machine.

Polk figures <small>1950-1954</small>

Frank Polk, a well-known artist depicting Western themes, designed the first of his figures around 1950. They were hand-carved and showed various Wild West figures, mostly incorporating Mills "Hi Top" slot machines. Original Polk figures are very expensive nowadays and were imitated by a number of manufacturers.

The Fox Bell Machine

The Chicago slot machine manufacturer Tom Skelly was a rather odd, permanently suspicious character. He appears never to have advertised his products in newspapers or brochures for fear of trouble with the law. This meant that no-one went to court, as nearly all slots were used for illegal gambling. Manufacturers shamelessly helped themselves to others' designs: some of the practices employed by slot machine companies make the Wild West look positively tame.

National Twin Jackpot Revamp Bell Machine

1933-1936

This very attractive art deco machine bears one of the most successful jackpot fronts of the 1930s apart from those of Rock-Ola and Pace. Even this distinctive front was being made by three different manufacturers simultaneously.

Victoria

Jackpot
Revamp Bell Machine

The "Victoria" line was first produced in 1932 as a response to Mills' "Silent Line." This machine has "Fortune Reelstrips" and a double jackpot.

This is another example of how Ed Pace pacified customers who were having technical problems with their machines. He simply changed the size of the front and then sold Watling exactly the same model as had already been selling to Mills and Jennings.

Gooseneck
Three Reel Slot
approx. 1935

This particular machine is
fitted with a Roberts
"Conversion Front."

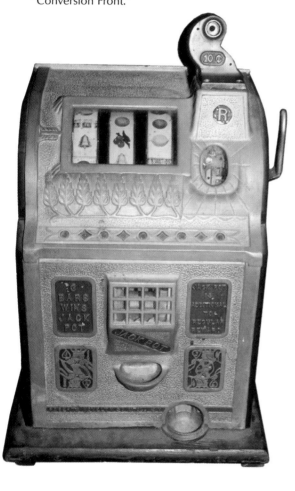

The Kelley approx. 1904

The cabinet of this little
machine from Chicago was
mainly made of oak. Its
operation was simple: if the
numbers on the reels added up
to the totals on the reward
cards, the machine paid out.
This model was also a stick
gum vendor.

Watling
Blue Seal
Twin Jackpot
1929-1935

A beautifully restored machine
in its original colors.

Mills
Golf Ball Vendor
Bell Console
1937-1941

This classic machine survived all the changing gambling laws and restrictions, and was still in use in the 1970s. It was often used in clubs, and no-one pretended it was anything other than a gambling machine. It was based on the 1933 Mills "Extraordinary," with the addition of a console and golf ball vendor. The machine contained between 100 and 150 balls and must have been the ideal machine for golf clubs.

Groetchen **Mercury Counter Game** 1939-1942

"Small Penny Cigarette Slots" were very popular in the late 1930s. The successful forerunner of the "Mercury" was the 1937 "Ginger Token Pay Out." The "Mercury" shown here was more streamlined in design than its predecessor, and paid out a token if three of the same cigarette symbols appeared in the window: this could be exchanged for up to ten packs of cigarettes. These counter models were made by Duval. If the manufacturer's plate is missing it is very hard to identify the machine exactly, as these were very widely copied. The "Mercury" Series" came in countless variations with different styling, and production ceased in the early 1940s.